White Privilege: Fact or Fiction

Prepared by

Meru El Muad'Dib

1828 Definition of American

AMER'ICAN, noun A native of America; **originally applied to the aboriginals, or copper-colored races, found here by the Europeans**; but now applied to the descendants of Europeans born in America.

An Invasion Disguised as Discovery

EARLY SETTLEMENTS

The early 1600s saw the beginning of **a great tide of emigration from Europe to North America**. Spanning more than three centuries, this movement grew from a trickle of a few hundred English colonists to a flood of millions of newcomers. Impelled by powerful and diverse motivations, they built a new civilization on the northern part of the continent.

The first English immigrants to what is now the United States crossed the Atlantic long after thriving Spanish colonies had been established in Mexico, the West Indies and South America. Like all early travelers to the New World, they came in small, overcrowded ships. During their six- to 12-week voyages, they lived on meager rations. Many died of disease; ships were often battered by storms and some were lost at sea.

Most European emigrants left their homelands to **escape political oppression**, to **seek the freedom to practice their religion**, or **for adventure and opportunities denied them at home**. Between 1620 and 1635, economic difficulties swept England. Many people could not find work. Even skilled artisans could earn little more than a bare living. Poor crop yields added to the distress. In addition, the Industrial Revolution had created a burgeoning textile industry, which demanded an ever-increasing supply of wool to keep the looms running. Landlords enclosed farmlands and evicted the peasants in favor of sheep cultivation. Colonial expansion became an outlet for this displaced peasant population.

The colonists' first glimpse of the new land was a vista of dense woods. **The settlers might not have survived had it not been for the help of friendly Indians, who taught them how to grow** native plants -- pumpkin, squash, beans and corn. In addition, the vast, virgin forests, extending nearly 2,100 kilometers along the Eastern seaboard, proved a rich source of game and firewood. **They also provided abundant raw materials used to build houses, furniture, ships and profitable cargoes for export**.

Although the new continent was remarkably endowed by nature, trade with Europe was vital for articles the settlers could not produce. The coast served the immigrants well. The whole length of shore provided innumerable inlets and harbors. Only two areas -- North Carolina and southern New Jersey -- lacked harbors for ocean-going vessels.

Majestic rivers -- the Kennebec, Hudson, Delaware, Susquehanna, Potomac and numerous others -- linked lands between the coast and the Appalachian Mountains with the sea. Only one river, however, the St. Lawrence -- dominated by the French in Canada -- offered a water passage to the Great Lakes and into the heart of the continent. Dense forests, the resistance of some Indian tribes and the formidable barrier of the Appalachian Mountains discouraged settlement beyond the coastal plain. Only trappers and traders ventured into the wilderness. **For the first hundred years the colonists built their settlements compactly along the coast**.

Political considerations influenced many people to move to America. In the 1630s, arbitrary rule by England's Charles I gave impetus to the migration to the New World. The subsequent revolt and triumph of Charles' opponents under Oliver Cromwell in the 1640s led many cavaliers -- "king's men" -- to cast their lot in Virginia. In the German-speaking regions of Europe, the oppressive policies of various petty princes -- particularly with regard to religion -- **and the devastation caused by a long**

series of wars helped swell the movement to America in the late 17th and 18th centuries.

The coming of colonists in the 17th century entailed careful planning and management, as well as considerable expense and risk. Settlers had to be transported nearly 5,000 kilometers across the sea. They needed utensils, clothing, seed, tools, building materials, livestock, arms and ammunition.

In contrast to the colonization policies of other countries and other periods, the emigration from England was not directly sponsored by the government **but by private groups of individuals whose chief motive was profit**.

JAMESTOWN

The first of the British colonies to take hold in North America was Jamestown. On the basis of a charter which King James I granted to the Virginia (or London) Company, a group of about 100 men set out for the Chesapeake Bay in 1607. Seeking to avoid conflict with the Spanish, they chose a site about 60 kilometers up the James River from the bay.

Made up of townsmen and adventurers more interested in finding gold than farming, **the group was unequipped by temperament or ability to embark upon a completely new life in the wilderness**. Among them, Captain John Smith emerged as the dominant figure. Despite quarrels, starvation and Indian attacks, his ability to enforce discipline held the little colony together through its first year.

In 1609 Smith returned to England, and in his absence, the colony descended into anarchy. During the winter of 1609-1610, the majority of the colonists succumbed to disease. Only 60 of the original 300 settlers were still alive by May 1610. That same year, the town of Henrico (now Richmond) was established farther up the James River.

It was not long, however, before a development occurred that revolutionized Virginia's economy. In 1612 John Rolfe began cross-breeding imported tobacco seed from the West Indies with native plants and produced a new variety that was pleasing to European taste. The first shipment of this tobacco reached London in 1614. Within a decade it had become Virginia's chief source of revenue.

Prosperity did not come quickly, however, and the death rate from disease and Indian attacks remained extraordinarily high. Between 1607 and 1624 approximately 14,000 people migrated to the colony, yet only 1,132 were living there in 1624. On recommendation of a royal commission, the king dissolved the Virginia Company, and made it a royal colony that year.

MASSACHUSETTS

During the religious upheavals of the 16th century, a body of men and women called Puritans sought to reform the Established Church of England from within. Essentially, they demanded that the rituals and structures associated with Roman Catholicism be replaced by simpler Protestant forms of faith and worship. Their reformist ideas, by destroying the unity of the state church, threatened to divide the people and to undermine royal authority.

In 1607 a small group of Separatists -- a radical sect of Puritans who did not believe the Established Church could ever be reformed -- departed for Leyden, Holland, where the Dutch granted them asylum. However, the Calvinist Dutch restricted them mainly to low-paid laboring jobs. Some members of the congregation grew dissatisfied with this discrimination and resolved to emigrate to the New World.

In 1620, a group of Leyden Puritans secured a land patent from the Virginia Company, and a group of 101 men, women and children set out for Virginia on board the *Mayflower*. A storm sent them far north and they landed in New England on Cape Cod. **Believing themselves outside the jurisdiction of any**

organized government, the men drafted a formal agreement to abide by "just and equal laws" drafted by leaders of their own choosing. This was the Mayflower Compact.

In December the Mayflower reached Plymouth harbor; the Pilgrims began to build their settlement during the winter. Nearly half the colonists died of exposure and disease, **but neighboring Wampanoag Indians provided information that would sustain them**: how to grow maize. By the next fall, the Pilgrims had a plentiful crop of corn, and a growing trade based on furs and lumber.

A new wave of immigrants arrived on the shores of Massachusetts Bay in 1630 bearing a grant from King Charles I to establish a colony. Many of them were **Puritans whose religious practices were increasingly prohibited** in England. Their leader, John Winthrop, openly set out to create a "city upon a hill" in the New World. By this he meant a place where Puritans would live in strict accordance with their religious beliefs.

The Massachusetts Bay Colony was to play a significant role in the development of the entire New England region, in part because Winthrop and his Puritan colleagues were able to bring their charter with them. Thus the authority for the colony's government resided in Massachusetts, not in England.

Under the charter's provisions, power rested with the General Court, which was made up of "freemen" required to be members of the Puritan Church. **This guaranteed that the Puritans would be the dominant political as well as religious force in the colony**. It was the General Court which elected the governor. For most of the next generation, this would be John Winthrop.

The rigid orthodoxy of the Puritan rule was not to everyone's liking. One of the first to challenge the General Court openly was a young clergyman named Roger Williams, who objected to the colony's seizure of Indian lands and its relations with the Church of England.

Banished from Massachusetts Bay, he purchased land from the Narragansett Indians in what is now Providence, Rhode Island, in 1636. There he set up the first American colony where complete separation of church and state as well as freedom of religion was practiced.

So-called heretics like Williams were not the only ones who left Massachusetts. Orthodox Puritans, seeking better lands and opportunities, soon began leaving Massachusetts Bay Colony. News of the fertility of the Connecticut River Valley, for instance, attracted the interest of farmers having a difficult time with poor land. By the early 1630s, many were ready to brave the danger of Indian attack to obtain level ground and deep, rich soil. These new communities often eliminated church membership as a prerequisite for voting, thereby extending the franchise to ever larger numbers of men.

At the same time, other settlements began cropping up along the New Hampshire and Maine coasts, as more and more immigrants sought the land and liberty the New World seemed to offer.

NEW NETHERLAND AND MARYLAND

Hired by the Dutch East India Company, Henry Hudson in 1609 explored the area around what is now New York City and the river that bears his name, to a point probably north of Albany, New York. Subsequent Dutch voyages laid the basis for their claims and early settlements in the area.

Like the French to the north, the first interest of the Dutch was the fur trade. To this end, the Dutch cultivated close relations with the Five Nations of the Iroquois who were the key to the heartland from which the furs came. In 1617 Dutch settlers built a fort at the junction of the Hudson and the Mohawk Rivers, where Albany now stands.

Settlement on the island of Manhattan began in the early 1620s. In 1624, the island was purchased from local Indians for the reported price of $24. It was promptly renamed New Amsterdam.

In order to attract settlers to the Hudson River region, the Dutch encouraged a type of feudal aristocracy, known as the "patroon" system. **The first of these huge estates** were established in 1630 along the Hudson River.

Under the **patroon system**, any stockholder, or patroon, who **could bring 50 adults to his estate over a four-year period was given a 25-kilometer river-front plot, exclusive fishing and hunting privileges, and civil and criminal jurisdiction over his lands**. In turn, he provided livestock, tools and buildings. The tenants paid the patroon rent and gave him first option on surplus crops.

Further to the south, a Swedish trading company with ties to the Dutch attempted to set up its first settlement along the Delaware River three years later. Without the resources to consolidate its position, New Sweden was gradually absorbed into New Netherland, and later, Pennsylvania and Delaware.

In 1632 the Calvert family obtained a charter for land north of the Potomac River from King Charles I in what became known as Maryland. As the charter did not expressly prohibit the establishment of non-Protestant churches, the family encouraged fellow Catholics to settle there. Maryland's first town, St. Mary's, was established in 1634 near where the Potomac River flows into the Chesapeake Bay.

While establishing a refuge for Catholics who were facing increasing persecution in Anglican England, the Calvert's were also interested in creating profitable estates. To this end, and to avoid trouble with the British government**, they also encouraged Protestant immigration**.

The royal charter granted to the Calvert family had a mixture of feudal and modern elements. On the one hand they had the power to create manorial estates. On the other, they could only make laws with the consent of freemen (property holders). They found that in order to attract settlers -- and make a profit from their holdings -- **they had to offer people farms**, not just tenancy on the manorial estates. The number of independent farms grew in consequence, and their owners demanded a voice in the affairs of the colony. Maryland's first legislature met in 1635.

COLONIAL-INDIAN RELATIONS

By 1640 the British had solid colonies established along the New England coast and the Chesapeake Bay. In between were the Dutch and the tiny Swedish community. To the west were the original Americans, the Indians.

Sometimes friendly, sometimes hostile, the Eastern tribes were no longer strangers to the Europeans. Although Native Americans benefitted from access to new technology and trade, the disease and thirst for land which the early settlers also brought posed a serious challenge to the Indian's long-established way of life.

At first, trade with the European settlers brought advantages: knives, axes, weapons, cooking utensils, fish hooks and a host of other goods. Those Indians who traded initially had significant advantage over rivals who did not.

In response to European demand, tribes such as the Iroquois began to devote more attention to fur trapping during the 17th century. Furs and pelts provided tribes the means to purchase colonial goods until late into the 18th century.

Early colonial-Indian relations were an uneasy mix of cooperation and conflict. On the one hand, there were the exemplary relations which prevailed during the first half century of Pennsylvania's existence. On the other were a long series of setbacks, skirmishes and wars, which almost invariably resulted in an Indian defeat and further loss of land.

The first of the important Indian uprisings occurred in Virginia in 1622, when some 347 whites were killed, including a number of missionaries who had just recently come to Jamestown. The Pequot War followed in 1637, as local tribes tried to prevent settlement of the Connecticut River region.

In 1675 Phillip, the son of the chief who had made the original peace with the Pilgrims in 1621, attempted to unite the tribes of southern New England against further European encroachment of their lands. In the struggle, however, Phillip lost his life and many Indians were sold into servitude.

Almost 5,000 kilometers to the west, the Pueblo Indians rose up against the Spanish missionaries five years later in the area around Taos, New Mexico. For the next dozen years the Pueblo controlled their former land again, only to see the Spanish retake it. Some 60 years later, another Indian revolt took place when the Pima Indians clashed with the Spanish in what is now Arizona.

The steady influx of settlers into the backwoods regions of the Eastern colonies disrupted Indian life. As more and more game was killed off, tribes were faced with the difficult choice of going hungry, going to war, or moving and coming into conflict with other tribes to the west.

The Iroquois, who inhabited the area below Lakes Ontario and Erie in northern New York and Pennsylvania, were more successful in resisting European advances. In 1570 five tribes joined to form the most democratic nation of its time, the "Ho-De-No-Sau-Nee," or League of the Iroquois. The League was run by a council made up of 50 representatives from each of the five member tribes. The council dealt with matters common to all the tribes, but it had no say in how the free and equal tribes ran their day-to-day affairs. No tribe was allowed to make war by itself. The council passed laws to deal with crimes such as murder.

The League was a strong power in the 1600s and 1700s. It traded furs with the British and sided with them against the French in the war for the dominance of America between 1754 and 1763. The British might not have won that war without the support of the League of the Iroquois.

The League stayed strong until the American Revolution. Then, for the first time, the council could not reach a unanimous decision on whom to support. Member tribes made their own decisions, some fighting with the British, some with the colonists, some remaining neutral. As a result, **everyone fought against the Iroquois**. Their losses were great and the League never recovered.

SECOND GENERATION OF BRITISH COLONIES

The religious and civil conflict in England in the mid-17th century limited immigration, as well as the attention the mother country paid the fledgling American colonies.

In part to provide for the defense measures England was neglecting, the Massachusetts Bay, Plymouth, Connecticut and New Haven colonies formed the New England Confederation in 1643. It was the European colonists' first attempt at regional unity.

The early history of the British settlers reveals a good deal of contention -- religious and political -- as groups vied for power and position among themselves and their neighbors. Maryland, in particular, suffered from the bitter religious rivalries which afflicted England during the era of Oliver Cromwell. One of the casualties was the state's Toleration Act, which was revoked in the 1650s. It was soon reinstated, however, along with the religious freedom it guaranteed.

In 1675 Bacon's Rebellion, the first significant revolt against royal authority, broke out in the colonies. The original spark was a clash between Virginia frontiersmen and the Susquehannock Indians, but it soon pitted the common farmer against the wealth and privilege of the large planters and Virginia's governor, William Berkeley.

The small farmers, embittered by low tobacco prices and hard living conditions, rallied around Nathaniel Bacon, a recent arrival from England. Berkeley refused to grant Bacon a commission to conduct Indian raids, but he did agree to call new elections to the House of Burgesses, which had remained unchanged since 1661.

Defying Berkeley's orders, Bacon led an attack against the friendly Ocaneechee tribe, **nearly wiping them out**. Returning to Jamestown in September 1676, he burned it, forcing Berkeley to flee. Most of the state was now under Bacon's control. His victory was short lived, however; he died of a fever the following month. Without Bacon, the rebellion soon lost its vitality. Berkeley re-established his authority and hanged 23 of Bacon's followers.

With the restoration of King Charles II in 1660, the British once again turned their attentions to North America. Within a brief span, the first European settlements were established in the Carolinas and the Dutch driven out of New Netherland. New proprietary colonies were established in New York, New Jersey, Delaware and Pennsylvania.

The Dutch settlements had, as a general matter, been ruled by autocratic governors appointed in Europe. Over the years, the local population had become estranged from them. As a result, when the British colonists began encroaching on Dutch lands in Long Island and Manhattan, the unpopular governor was unable to rally the population to their defense. New Netherland fell in 1664. The terms of the capitulation, however, were mild: the Dutch settlers were able to retain their property and worship as they pleased.

As early as the 1650s, the Ablemarle Sound region off the coast of what is now northern North Carolina was inhabited by settlers trickling down from Virginia. The first proprietary governor arrived in 1664. A remote area even today, Ablemarle's first town was not established until the arrival of a group of French Huguenots in 1704.

In 1670 the first settlers, drawn from New England and the Caribbean island of Barbados, arrived in what is now Charleston, South Carolina. An elaborate system of government, to which the British philosopher John Locke contributed, was prepared for the new colony. One of its prominent features was a failed attempt to create a hereditary nobility. **One of the colony's least appealing aspects was the early trade in Indian slaves**. Within time, however, timber, rice and indigo gave the colony a worthier economic base.

Massachusetts Bay was not the only colony driven by religious motives. In 1681 William Penn, a wealthy Quaker and friend of Charles II, received a large tract of land west of the Delaware River, which became known as Pennsylvania. **To help populate it, Penn actively recruited a host of religious dissenters from England and the continent -- Quakers, Mennonites, Amish, Moravians and Baptists**.

When Penn arrived the following year, there were already Dutch, Swedish and English settlers living along the Delaware River. It was there he founded Philadelphia, the "City of Brotherly Love."

In keeping with his faith, Penn was motivated by a sense of equality not often found in other American colonies at the time. Thus, women in Pennsylvania had rights long before they did in other parts of America. Penn and his deputies also paid considerable attention to the colony's relations with the Delaware Indians, ensuring that they were paid for any land the Europeans settled on.

Georgia was settled in 1732, the last of the 13 colonies to be established. Lying close to, if not actually inside the boundaries of Spanish Florida, the region was viewed as a buffer against Spanish incursion. But it had another unique quality: the man charged with Georgia's fortifications, General James Oglethorpe, was a reformer who deliberately set out to create a refuge where the poor and former prisoners would be given new opportunities.

https://usa.usembassy.de/etexts/history/ch1.htm

SETTLERS, SLAVES AND SERVANTS

Men and women with little active interest in a new life in America **were often induced to make the move to the New World by the skillful persuasion of promoters**. William Penn, for example, publicized the opportunities awaiting newcomers to the Pennsylvania colony. Judges and prison authorities offered convicts a chance to migrate to colonies like Georgia instead of serving prison sentences.

But few colonists could finance the cost of passage for themselves and their families to make a start in the new land. In some cases, ships' captains received large rewards from the sale of service contracts for poor migrants, called indentured servants, and every method from extravagant promises to actual kidnapping was used to take on as many passengers as their vessels could hold.

In other cases, the expenses of transportation and maintenance were paid by colonizing agencies like the Virginia or Massachusetts Bay Companies. In return, indentured servants agreed to work for the agencies as contract laborers, usually for four to seven years. Free at the end of this term, they would be given "freedom dues," sometimes including a small tract of land.

It has been estimated that half the settlers living in the colonies south of New England came to America under this system. Although most of them fulfilled their obligations faithfully, some ran away from their employers. Nevertheless, **many of them were eventually able to secure land and set up homesteads**, either in the colonies in which they had originally settled or in neighboring ones. No social stigma was attached to a family that had its beginning in America under this semi-bondage. Every colony had its share of leaders who were former indentured servants.

There was one very important exception to this pattern: African slaves. The first blacks were brought to Virginia in 1619, just 12 years after the founding of Jamestown. Initially, many were regarded as indentured servants who could earn their freedom. By the 1660s, however, as the demand for plantation labor in the Southern colonies grew, the institution of slavery began to harden around them, and Africans were brought to America in shackles for a lifetime of involuntary servitude.

https://usa.usembassy.de/etexts/history/ch1.htm

The primary motivations for European immigrant to come to the Americas was, political, work or better jobs (better opportunities), freedom of religion, or just better overall conditions. Inherently, there isn't anything wrong so far; but when these are at the expense of another society or culture, it should never happen.

The process began to demand more workers for farming and agriculture. More people were needed to push the expansion westward. These demands were met by willing Europeans who were more than willing to accommodate their European American cousins, to populate stolen lands with additional benefits.

The patroon system, similar to the headright system (discussed in a later chapter), gave European immigrants assistance in getting a good foundation to start in this country.

"Until the 1920s, we had virtually an open door — **from Europe that is** — into the United States," she said.

Before the 1920s, **several successive waves of European immigration, starting with colonizers in the 16th century, moved to North America with little impediment beyond the steep price of passage.**

In the mid-1800s, the U.S. began asking newcomers from Europe more questions. However, Ngai said, this weeding out process was still minimal.

"They wanted to make sure you had a little cash in your pocket, so you wouldn't become a public charge, they wanted to make sure you didn't have what was called a 'dangerous or loathsome disease,' they wanted to make sure you weren't a prostitute," she said.

Even with a low bar, some European immigrants disguised their identities or reasons for coming.

In the late 19th century, immigration from Europe to the U.S. shifted — where there had been large influxes from England and Northern Europe, now more Southern and Eastern Europeans were moving to America. For the next 50 years, more than 20 million Europeans streamed through that "open door." Meanwhile, the U.S. had started banning entire groups of people, based on their race.

After a trip back to Ireland a few years later, White said, his grandfather committed another immigration crime **— lying on official paperwork to return to the United States**.

"Virtually everything on [his citizenship petition] except for his name is either a lie or wrong," said White, who wrote a book about his family's dodgy immigration record. "He even has his own birthday wrong."

There is no reliable way to know how many people sneaked into the U.S. or lied on official documents during this period, according to White. Later, laws granting amnesty such as the Registry Act of 1929 indicate that hundreds of thousands of European immigrants came into the U.S. through unofficial channels, or simply lost their documents, and became citizens.

https://whyy.org/segments/did-european-immigrants-come-to-the-u-s-the-right-way/

Many European immigrants benefited from "amnesties."

Acknowledging the large numbers of Europeans in the United States without proper authorization, the government devised ways for them to remain in the country legally. The 1929 Registry Act allowed "honest law-abiding alien[s] who may be in the country under some merely technical irregularity" to register as permanent residents for a fee of $20 if they could prove they had lived in the country since 1921 and were of "good moral character." Roughly 115,000 immigrants registered between 1930 and 1940—80% were European or Canadian. Between 1925 and 1965, 200,000 unauthorized Europeans legalized their status through the Registry Act, through "pre-examination"—a process that allowed them to leave the United States voluntarily and re-enter legally with a visa (a "touch-back" program), or through discretionary rules that allowed immigration officials to suspend deportations in "meritorious" cases. In the 1940s and 1950s, several thousand deportations a year were suspended; approximately 73% of those who benefitted were Europeans (mostly Germans and Italians).

https://www.americanimmigrationcouncil.org/research/did-my-family-really-come-legally-todays-immigration-laws-created-a-new-reality

The Headright System

Imagine if you were given 50 acres of land for a person you sponsored to come to the United States! This sounds like it could turn out to be pretty profitable.

The **headright system** referred to a grant of land, usually 50 acres, given to settlers in the 13 colonies. The system was used mainly in Virginia, Georgia, North Carolina, South Carolina, and Maryland. It proved to be quite effective by increasing the population in the British colonies.

The headright system was originally created in 1618 in Jamestown, Virginia. It was used as a way to attract new settlers to the region and address the labor shortage. With the emergence of tobacco farming, a large supply of workers was needed. New settlers who paid their way to Virginia received 50 acres of land. However, most of the workers who arrived in Virginia were indentured servants, people who pledged to perform five to seven years of labor.

Many families grew in power by receiving many acres of land. One landowner purchased 60 slaves and received 3,000 acres of land in 1638. The more land a family acquired, the wealthier they became overnight. This eventually led to land only being distributed for **settlers from England**, and no longer slaves from Africa.

https://study.com/academy/lesson/headright-system-definition-lesson-quiz.html

The early inhabitants of Jamestown were employees of the Virginia Company and were supposed to direct their labors toward the production of profits for the investors. It quickly became apparent that gold and silver did not exist in appreciable amounts in eastern North America, a fact that left the colony without a cash crop and the resultant threat of bankruptcy.

The advent of the tobacco economy in the 1610s changed the course of Virginia's development. Tobacco production required large tracts of land and many workers. The company held title to tremendous amounts of land, but had few workers at their disposal.

In 1618, the headright system was introduced as a means to solve the labor shortage. It provided the following:

- Colonists already residing in Virginia were granted two headrights, meaning two tracts of 50 acres each, or a total of 100 acres of land.

- New settlers who paid their own passage to Virginia were granted one headright. Since every person who entered the colony received a headright, families were encouraged to migrate together.
- Wealthy individuals could accumulate headrights by paying for the passage of poor individuals. Most of the workers who entered Virginia under this arrangement came as indentured servants — people who paid for their transportation by pledging to perform five to seven years of labor for the landowner. **The ability to amass large plots of land by importing workers provided the basis for an emerging aristocracy in Virginia**. Plantation owners were further enriched by receiving headrights for newly imported slaves.

The implementation of the headright system was an important ingredient in Virginia's success. Land ownership gave many people a reason to work hard, with the assurance that they were providing for their own futures, not that of the company.

Georgia headright grants land came power. Georgia was faced with hostile Creek and Cherokee Indians, and the headright system seemed to be the perfect solution. By granting lands to settlers they would build a buffer zone around the state on the bathe headright system seemed to be the perfect solution.

https://www.u-s-history.com/pages/h1153.html

The headright system encouraged people to **migrate to America in large numbers** with their families because **the more people they brought over the more land they would get**. Any person in America who paid for the voyage of another person to America would get an additional headright. These people were called indentured servants (work the land for 3-5 years). **Some colonists were able to form small plantations**. **This encouraged the prosperous to bring new laborers to**

America. Some colonists were able to make small plantations. In return they would contribute 1 shilling a year for each headright to the company.

https://quizlet.com/10672431/history-7a-chapter-2-flash-cards/

The headright system allowed for poorer people to come to the New World who otherwise would not have been able to afford it. The system was incredibly important to the growth of the colonies, especially in the South. Tobacco farming, especially, required large tracts of land and many workers. The headright system allowed this to develop relatively quickly.

https://magoosh.com/hs/apush/2017/headright-system-apush/

In addition to leading to the distribution of too much land at the lax secretary's discretion, the headright system increased tensions between Native Americans and colonists. Indentured servants were granted land inland, which was near the natives. This migration produced conflict between the natives and the indentured servants.

https://en.wikipedia.org/wiki/Headright

The pre-existing ownership rights of the Native Americans, the current occupants, were dismissed. At various times the English stated simply that they owned the land through "right of discovery" and "right of conquest." Treaties were negotiated with different tribes in the 1600's and 1700's to extinguish Native American claims, but land was seized rather than purchased from the original inhabitants.

http://www.virginiaplaces.org/settleland/headright.html

The headright system was not only very profitable, it greatly increased the number of European immigrants to North America.

Would those same families that rose to aristocracy in Virginia achieve the same status without the help of the headright? Was that not an advantage as well? Once again, the land was not theirs to give away! This is another instance of stolen land given away to European immigrants.

It would be safe to assume that some of those plantations acquired by European immigrants, were later on, worked by African slaves or Aboriginal American slaves as well.

The headright system offered a way for poor Europeans to come to America and be successful after a short indentured servant period. They were guaranteed land and rights the Aboriginal American was denied.

Natural Or Not

Naturalization- the admittance of a foreigner to the citizenship of a country.

The original United States Naturalization Law of March 26, 1790 (1 Stat. 103) provided the first rules to be followed by the United States in the granting of national citizenship. This law limited naturalization to **immigrants** who were free White persons of good character.

Google.com

The original United States Naturalization Law of March 26, 1790 (1 Stat. 103) provided the first rules to be followed by the United States in the granting of national citizenship. This law limited naturalization to **immigrants** who were free White persons of good character. It thus excluded Native Americans, indentured servants, slaves, free blacks and later Asians, although free blacks were allowed citizenship at the state level in certain states. It also provided for citizenship for the children of U.S. citizens born abroad, stating that such children "shall be considered as natural born citizens," the only US statute ever to use the term. It specified that the right of citizenship did "not descend to persons whose fathers have never been resident in the United States.

https://en.wikipedia.org/wiki/Naturalization_Act_of_1790

The history of U.S. immigration and nationality law demonstrates how race became a factor in determining who could come to America and who could not. Studies of Chinese exclusion laws or the old immigration "quota system**" trace a tradition of racist immigration policy**. The Supreme Court reinforced this policy in the 1920s with a decision stating that Americans shared a "common understanding" of who was and was not "white," and by extension shared a "common understanding" of who did and did not belong in the United States.

As the nation marched west**, a regular supply of immigrants from Europe arrived to occupy new territories** and hold them for their new nation.

Nationality law allowed for political inclusion of new arrivals into the United States. Between 1790 and 1802, Congress established simple rules for naturalization and facilitated the process by granting naturalization authority— which belonged originally to the legislative branch— to "any court of record." Naturalization requirements included five years' residence in the country, "good moral character," and that applicants be "free white persons." Such language in 1802 preserved the constitutional understanding of citizens as **white persons** and exclusion of African Americans and "Indians not taxed" from citizenship. U.S. nationality law generally **transformed northern and western European immigrants into U.S. citizens**. **For most of the nineteenth century, Europe was the primary source of immigration to the United States**, and it no doubt seemed the law would be adequate forever.

https://www.archives.gov/publications/prologue/2002/summer/immigration-law-1.html

Indian Removal Act

The Indian Removal Act was signed into law by President Andrew Jackson on May 28, 1830, authorizing the president to grant unsettled lands west of the Mississippi in exchange for Indian lands within existing state borders. A few tribes went peacefully, but many resisted the relocation policy. During the fall and winter of 1838 and 1839, the Cherokees were forcibly moved west by the United States government. Approximately 4,000 Cherokees died on this forced march, which became known as the "Trail of Tears."

https://guides.loc.gov/indian-removal-act

Christian missionaries protested the Indian Removal Act, but the majority of those living in the South wanted it to pass so **that they could then inhabit their land**. There was also the belief that there was gold to be found where the Native tribes lived.

Gold was discovered in Georgia in 1828, which sped up the passing of the Indian Removal Act. The 'Five Civilized Tribes' inhabited the land in Georgia where gold was found.

The 'Five Civilized Tribes' included the Chickasaw, the Choctaw, the Muscogee-Creek, the Seminole, and Cherokee Nations.

Other Native tribes that were affected by the Indian Removal Act included the Wyandot, the Kickapoo, the Lenape, the Shawnee, and the Potowatomi tribes.

The Five Civilized Tribes had adopted Anglo-American practices, such as farming, western education practices, and even slavery in an effort to assimilate with the settlers in a peaceful manner. **This did not work as the settlers became hostile and resentful**.

http://www.softschools.com/facts/us_history/indian_removal_act_facts/2832/

It is generally acknowledged that this act spelled the end of Indian Rights to live in those states under their own traditional laws. They were forced to assimilate and concede to US law or leave their homelands. The Indian Nations themselves were force to move and ended up in Oklahoma.

The great Cherokee Nation that had fought the young Andrew Jackson back in 1788 now faced an even more powerful and determined man who was intent on taking their land. But where in the past they had resorted to guns, tomahawks, and scalping knives, now they chose to challenge him in a court of law. They were not called a 'civilized nation' for nothing. Many of their leaders were well educated; many more could read and write; they had their own written language, thanks to Sequoyah, a constitution, schools, and their own newspaper. And they had adopted many skills of the white man to improve their living conditions. Why should they be expelled from their lands when they no longer threatened white settlements and could compete with them on many levels? They intended to fight their ouster, and they figured they had many ways to do it. As a last resort they planned to bring suit before the Supreme Court.

Prior to that action, they sent a delegation to Washington to plead their cause. They petitioned Congress to protect them against the unjust laws of Georgia that had decreed that they were subject to its sovereignty and under its complete jurisdiction. They even approached the President, but he curtly informed them that there was nothing he could do in their quarrel with the state, a statement that shocked and amazed them.

So the Cherokees hired William Wirt to take their case to the Supreme Court. In the celebrated Cherokee Nation v. Georgia he instituted suit for an injunction that would permit the Cherokees to remain in Georgia without interference by the state. He argued that they constituted an independent nation and had been so regarded by the United States in its many treaties with them.

Speaking for the majority of the court, Chief Justice John Marshall handed down his decision on March 18, 1831. Not surprisingly, as a great American nationalist, he rejected Wirt's argument that the Cherokees were a sovereign nation, but he also rejected Jackson's claim that they were subject to state law. **The Indians were 'domestic dependent nations**,' he ruled, **subject to the United States as a ward to a guardian**. Indian territory was part of the United States but not subject to action by individual states.

https://www.historynet.com/indian-removal-act

This result was due to the disastrous **Doctrine of Discovery**; (see my 3 book series on the topic) which stated that because there weren't any Christians in the America's when the European nations came to conquer, the land was uninhabited and therefore open to be 'discovered' and claimed by the conquering European nation.

At the same time, the Aboriginal American tribes were reduced to second-class citizens and their tribes forced to dependent nations, dependent upon the United States government. This is why the Cherokee's (Kitoowah) lost in court. Most people aren't aware of the Doctrine of Discovery. This is the reason why most Aboriginal Americans (blacks, negroes, colored, African-American) suffer the way we do. (see the second and third book in the Doctrine of Discovery series)

Jackson's attitude toward Native Americans was paternalistic and patronizing -- he described them as children in need of guidance. and believed the removal policy was beneficial to the Indians.

Most white Americans thought that the United States would never extend beyond the Mississippi. Removal would save Indian people from the depredations of whites, and would resettle them in an area where they could govern themselves in peace. But some Americans saw this as an excuse for a brutal and inhumane course of action, and protested loudly against removal.

https://www.pbs.org/wgbh/aia/part4/4p2959.html

The beginning of the end for the so-called Five Civilized Tribes began in 1830 with their removal signed and sealed. It can clearly be seen, the Aboriginal American was being removed to make way for the coming European immigrants who were soon to be invited to take ownership of the lands left by the Aboriginal Americans. Displace the original people and soon the invite goes out to their replacements.

How can this not be an advantage for the people who arrived to take ownership over land they didn't have any rights to or earned? Their way to America was paved with the Trail of Tears.

Brief Stop On the Trail

In the year 1838, 16,000 Native Americans were marched over 1,200 miles of rugged land. Over 4,000 of these Indians died of disease, famine, and warfare. The Indian tribe was called the Cherokee and we call this event the Trail of Tears. As you will soon learn, it is one of the most brutal and racist events to happen in America.

The Trail of Tears happened when Hernando De Soto took his adventures to America. After he came to America more and more Europeans came and began to invade on Indian land. The Indians became lost in bewilderment and anger. Some tribes didn't feel this way until later on, for some helped the new comers win wars during the colonial periods. Often when the Indians' side lost the war, the Indians would have to give up a large portion of their land. So as you can see the greed for Indian Territory started early.

As we get back to the Trail of Tears you will learn that there were many treaties signed between 1684 and 1835. Every treaty was broken, however, because of discoveries of gold on Indian territory.

In 1830 congress passed the Indian Removal Act because gold was discovered on Cherokee land. **Whites wanted the Indians out of the way**. President Andrew Jackson said,"The Indian Removal Act **will place a dense population in large tracts of the country now occupied by a few savage hunters**."

http://www.kawvalley.k12.ks.us/schools/rjh/marneyg/archived_projects/02_plains-history/02_masseyd_reportTOT.html

Who were these people who were to make up that "dense population," President Jackson was referring to? What was their nationality? Would it be safe to say that he was referring to Europeans?

The Cherokee Removal Forts are not as well known in the aspect of the Trail of Tears, They are overshadowed by the long journey itself. Over fifteen of the of these forts were located in Georgia alone.

The camps were filled with human waste and many women and children were raped. To make things worse on top of all that, the round up took over five months to complete; which was quite a bit longer than expected. Approximately one third of the deaths attributed to the trail of tears are a result of these forts. Many of these diseased camps have been lost to our history books.

A Georgia soldier once wrote in his journal, “I fought in many wars between the states and have seen many men killed, some by my own hands, but the Cherokee Removal was the **cruelest work I ever knew**.”

http://www.kawvalley.k12.ks.us/schools/rjh/marneyg/archived_projects/02_plains-history/02_masseyd_reportTOT.html

It is difficult to imagine the hardships, which the people of the Cherokee nation who made the forced march to the Indian Territory had to face.

Most of them hoped that the government would not force them to leave and made no plans for the long journey. When the government roundup of Cherokee began, many were forced from their homes with only the barest possessions. 16 000 Cherokee were divided into 16 detachments of about 1000 each.

Three groups left in June of 1838 travelling by rail, boat, and wagon primarily on the Water Route. But the detachments found themselves making the journey in the hottest part of the year when the river levels were too low for navigation.

Under the generally indifferent army commanders, human losses for these first groups of Cherokee removed were extremely high. Sickness and death rates caused by drought, bad water, bad diet and physical exhaustion were especially high among children. Some of the Cherokee left almost naked and without shoes or only in moccasins and refused government clothing because they felt it would be taken as an acceptance of being removed from their homes. Some refused government food; others were given food that they were not normally part of their diet, such as wheat flour, which they did not know how to use. One military estimate of the death in one of the parties was put at 17,7 %, with half of the dead being children.

15 000 captives still awaited removal. Poor sanitation and drought made them miserable. Many of them died. Chief Ross and The National Council of Cherokee appealed to General Scott to permit the rest of the Cherokee to wait until fall to move, and to supervise their own removal. General Scott approved the plan and Ross administrated the effort. The Cherokee were moved from removal forts to interment camps until travel resumed.

Although the last parties under Ross left in early fall and arrived in Oklahoma during the brutal winter of 1838-39, he significantly reduced the loss of life among his people. Twelve detachments of the Principal People which left in November, travelled to Indian Territory overland on existing roads across Tennessee, Kentucky, Illinois and Missouri. One detachment was lead by the Rev. Jesse Bushyhead and his Cherokee wife. He had been brought up within the culture of the Indians, and became a leader among Cherokee in their struggle against the white man's intrusion.

These detachments also met many hardships on their 1200 miles long journey to the west. Heavy rains turned the primitive roads to mud, and the Cherokee were often forced to manually drag the wagons out of the mud. Supplies of food were of poor quality. Road conditions, illness, and the distress of winter, made death a daily occurrence.

Two thirds of the ill-equipped Cherokee that were trapped beside the frozen Mississippi River still remembered a half-century later the hundreds of sick and dying in wagons or lying on the frozen ground with only a single blanket provided by the government to each Indian for shelter from the cold wind. Falling temperatures caused the surface of the river to freeze before all the detachments could be ferried across. The ice prevented both boat and horses from moving. Besides the cold, there was starvation and malnutrition. Weakened by the hunger, the Cherokee became easy victims of disease, particularly cholera, smallpox and dysentery. Many died on both sides of the river waiting for journey to resume. Quatie Ross, the Chief Ross' wife, gave her only blanket to a child and died of pneumonia.

https://www.univie.ac.at/Anglistik/webprojects/LiveMiss/TrailofTears/trailparent.htm

Scott Free

In March of 1857, the United States Supreme Court, led by Chief Justice Roger B. Taney, **declared that all blacks -- slaves as well as free -- were not and could never become citizens of the United States**. The court also declared the 1820 Missouri Compromise unconstitutional, thus permitting slavery in all of the country's territories.

The case before the court was that of Dred Scott v. Sanford. Dred Scott, a slave who had lived in the free state of Illinois and the free territory of Wisconsin before moving back to the slave state of Missouri, had appealed to the Supreme Court in hopes of being granted his freedom.

Taney -- a staunch supporter of slavery and intent on protecting southerners from northern aggression -- wrote in the Court's majority opinion that, **because Scott was black, he was not a citizen and therefore had no right to sue**. The framers of the Constitution, he wrote, **believed that blacks "had no rights which the white man was bound to respect**; **and that the negro might justly and lawfully be reduced to slavery for his benefit. He was bought and sold and treated as an ordinary article of merchandise and traffic, whenever profit could be made by it**."

http://www.pbs.org/wgbh/aia/part4/4h2933.html

In the opinion of the Court the legislation and histories of the times, and the language used in the Declaration of Independence, show that **neither the class of persons who had been imported as slaves nor their descendants, whether they had become free or not, were then acknowledged as a part of the people nor intended to be included in the general words used in that memorable instrument**....

They had for more than a century before been regarded as beings of an inferior order and altogether unfit to associate with the white race, either in social or political relations; and so far inferior that they had no rights which the white man was bound to respect; and that the Negro might justly and lawfully be reduced to slavery for his benefit. He was bought and sold and treated as an ordinary article of merchandise and traffic whenever a profit could be made by it. This opinion was at that time fixed and universal in the civilized portion of the white race....

No one, we presume, supposes that any change in public opinion or feeling, in relation to this unfortunate race, in the civilized nations of Europe or in this country should induce the Court to give to the words of the Constitution a more liberal construction in their favor than they were intended to bear when the instrument was framed and adopted....

And upon a full and careful consideration of the subject, the Court is of opinion that, upon the facts stated in the plea in abatement, Dred Scott was not a citizen of Missouri within the meaning of the Constitution of the United States and not entitled as such to sue in its courts....

http://www.digitalhistory.uh.edu/disp_textbook.cfm?smtID=3&psid=293

In the Doctrine of Discovery series, I discussed how Aboriginal Americans through the United States census, had misnomers applied to them. They were black, slaves, coloreds, octaroons, quadroons, then eventually African-American. So in essence, we see a very clever trick played here. With the new label applied to Dred Scott, (black, slave) the result is loss of citizenship, nationality, and status.

By accepting these inferior labels, people subject themselves to the same treatment and standing in law.

We have already seen how at almost every attempt was made to invite and even under shady circumstances, ways to give the European immigrant the legal standing and its advantages lawfully entitled to the Aboriginal Americans. They were unlawfully stripped of their birthrights and all that entails. While they were illegally passed on to an undeserving foreigner by people who had no right to give it away.

The Homestead Act

The Homestead Act of 1862 is universally recognized as a land law. The 37th Congress of the United States designed this legislation to **distribute the available public lands to private individuals**. **People could receive free title to 160 acres if they were willing to live on, cultivate and improve the land**. It is an undeniable fact, regardless of its perceived effectiveness, that the goal was to distribute land, thus **making it a land law**. However, it was much more. In fact, **the Homestead Act was the first accommodating immigration law**; **providing all necessary requirements for citizenship to individuals wanting to come homestead the public lands of the United Sates**. By examining the Congressional Debates and studying the language used in the narrative of the Homestead Act, it becomes apparent that the 37th Congress intended to use the Homestead Act as a way to build an agricultural nation by **encouraging immigrants to settle the public lands of the United States**.

After secession, the 37th Congress was overwhelmingly occupied by Lincoln-Republicans. In fact, there were 42 Representatives left in the house, of those 31 were Lincoln-Republicans, seven were Democrats, and four were members of the Constitutional Union Party. It is no surprise that the House Republicans would move to encourage a Homestead Act considering the National Party Platform issued at the Republican National Convention on May 17, 1860 clearly stated in item #13 that the party "protested against any sale or alienation to others of the Public Lands held by actual settlers, and against any view of the Free Homestead policy which regards the settlers as paupers or suppliants for public bounty; and we demand the passage by Congress of the complete and satisfactory Homestead Measure which has already passed the House." While most were in agreement that the western territories should be opened for homesteading the timing of the legislation was an issue because many viewed the public lands as a source of collateral for the public debt. In addition, the question of who could homestead was at the forefront. **Was it going to be for American Citizens only? Or were immigrants going to be allowed to participate**? **If immigrants were going to be allowed, what rules were going to be instituted to govern their ability to participate**?

However, with the Civil War in full scale, some northern congressmen saw the public lands as collateral for the debts they were incurring from the cost of war. A new faction of hardliners opposing the Homestead Act emerged led by then Congressman

Justin Morrill from Vermont. He articulated this new opposing viewpoint when he argued, "It must be admitted that here at home, among our own financiers, as well as among those abroad, the public lands are a resource that is relied upon as a security for the payment of our public debt." And to consider the Homestead Law during a time of war was a "suicidal policy". Wisconsin Congressman John Potter, head of the Committee for Public Lands was surprised to find opposition to the Homestead Act by those who had once supported its passage. He scolded the opposition saying:

I hope those gentlemen who have been friends of the homestead policy, who have in years gone by advocated that policy will not shrink from accepting it now that it is within our reach. We know the source of the opposition to this bill. We know from whence has proceeded such opposition heretofore. It is from the very men who are now engaged in a wicked rebellion against the Government... I am sorry that there should be any person in this House opposed to this rebellion and opposed to land monopolies that will stand up here and ask that this beneficent measure shall be postponed.

Congressman Isaac Newton Arnold from Illinois was among the most adamant defenders of the Homestead Act, and in pushing for its consideration after Congressman Potter, he said:

I urge the early passage of the homestead bill as a matter of importance in promoting the public credit, and providing the means of meeting the extraordinary expenses which the present condition of the country demand. The public domain has never been the source of any very large amount of revenue to the Treasury. I believe that it never will, so long as it remains unoccupied and uncultivated, be the source of any very large amount of public revenue. In my judgment, the best mode of making them productive, and to add to the security which the country can afford to those who loan her money at the present time, will be to invite settlement at as early a day as practicable.

... If they remain in their present condition they will neither add to the wealth nor the prosperity of the country, nor will they add to the revenue of the country. But there are those ready to go upon those public lands, **there are the immigrants from the old world ready**, so soon as you pass this homestead bill, to go upon these wild lands, and to convert them into productive farms, by which the aggregate wealth of the country will be largely increased. Congressman Arnold saw production on the public lands as being the source of revenue, and he thought a "**liberal policy of the homestead bill**" **should be adopted to invite immigration to the west**; at which point the population increase would create new towns, cities, and eventually states.

Congressman Arnold"s argument was an ambitious desire to use the Homestead Act as an invitation to potential settlers in the "old world". Congressman William Kelley from Pennsylvania supported Congressman Arnold"s pro-immigration stance with respect to homesteading. He argued that, "**Bread is high**, **employment scarce**, **wages are low in Europe**, **and there will be a tide of men flowing into our country that will give value to those lands**." He continued poetically:

Let the people of Europe see that the patriotic people of the country are carrying on the ordinary pursuits of life notwithstanding the abstraction of half a million of men from their number; let them see that the glorious deeds of our Navy are followed up by prompt and well-directed blows from the Army; and **there will come from Britain and from all Europe a flow of men that will give to the Northwest population and to the country revenue from its lands**.

Not all congressmen were as convinced as Congressman Kelley that immigrants were going to come and generate the wealth from the public lands needed to fund the war, but **many were open to the idea of immigrants being allowed to claim homesteads in the event that the legislation passed**.

Congressman William Vandever from Iowa was convinced that populating the public lands would increase the wealth and security of the United States, and **he understood that immigration was a valuable resource to ensure the success of settlement in the West**. He claimed that if the public lands are opened to actual settlers that a "tide of immigration will pour in upon them, and the settlement and occupation of them will increase immeasurably the basis of credit of the Government."10 And by transferring the public lands to private citizens; creditors could not call upon the U.S. government to sell the public lands; instead the taxes generated by cultivation would be the source of revenue needed to pay public debts. Giving away land is quiet an incentive for **potential immigrants**, distributing it indiscriminately does not ensure that the immigrant will become a citizen.

It is important to note that Congressman Vandever used the term "private citizen". **According to the naturalization laws immigrants would not be private U.S. citizens until they had declared their intentions to become a citizen and lived in the U.S. for a period of five years**. But by examining the language and requirements of the Homestead Act, all the requirements of naturalization are met.

In the first section of the Homestead Act it states, "That any person who is… a citizen of the United States, or who shall have filed his declaration of intention to become such" is entitled to file a claim. The argument that a person does not know the naturalization law is irrelevant to potential immigrant homesteaders because in order to file a claim they would have to declare their intentions to become a citizen.

In that respect the Homestead Act took care of the first criteria of **naturalization**. Secondly, **potential citizens were required to live in the U.S. for five years**. The Homestead Act also provides for this requirement in section two; "No certificate shall be given or patent issued therefor until the expiration of five years from date of such entry." In short, **in order to receive the land, claimants had to live on and cultivate the land for five years, the exact amount of time required to become a U.S. citizen**. **The Homestead Act becomes an accommodating immigration law by providing a credible reason to enter the United States, it ensured the criteria of the naturalization laws were met, and it ensured immigrants becoming citizens were exposed to and would adhere to the Constitution and its principals**.

The Homestead Act was the first piece of legislation to include all the necessary components to be considered an accommodating immigration law. The Act did not exclude any person based on race, gender, or nationality. In addition, it provides, within the language of the law, everything required of immigrants to become naturalized citizens. Congressman Potter understood this component of the Homestead Act and vehemently **argued for immigrants to have access to land in the United States under the legislation**. He said:

Immigration has almost ceased, and the present unsettled condition of Europe, tending to a general war on that continent, should invite, on our part, the adoption of the most liberal policy, which will induce the immigrant to seek a home here, and invest his capital and direct his labor to the development of the now unproductive resources of the

country. ...We shall do all in our power to invite immigration and capital to our unoccupied public lands.

On May 17, 1862 word of the impending passage of the Homestead Act and the possibility of a railroad coming through Kansas, the Big Blue Union newspaper in Marysville, Kansas reported, "Never again shall we have to appeal for immigration or ask from generous hearts the help demanded by a new and famine stricken people." The same article claimed that these laws would "be of incalculable advantage to Kansas." **Less than a month after the passage of the Homestead Act, the New York Times reported that immigration has increased after being stagnant and experiencing decline**.

The article said:

Europeans have learned of the immense extent of our country and its limitless resources... They have also begun, or soon will begin, to learn of the Homestead law, and provisions for securing to every man not only life, liberty and the freedom to pursue happiness but also the means of gaining an independent livelihood.

In November of 1862, Robert Walker, respected economist, former Senator, and fourth Territorial Governor of Kansas, **wrote of the benefit the Homestead Act would offer the European immigrant. He notes the annual price of rent for a single acre in England exceeds the price to file the paperwork and own 160 acres of land in America. Furthermore the Homestead Act provided the option to grow choice crops, live in desirable locations, and pick the neighbors they wanted to live near. He called on those being refused suffrage, toiling without ownership, bound by poverty and refused education to come to America and claim land under the Homestead Act. Here they could have "freedom, competence, the right of**

suffrage, the homestead farm, and free schools for his children."

Many members of congress and those in the general public saw the vast expanses of the West as having inexhaustible resources, room for all, **and the potential to build a stronger nation through immigration** and agriculture. **Westward expansion it was believed by many would encourage overcrowded cities in both Europe and America to send their surplus west**. **Impoverished immigrants looking for opportunity could find it out west.** The previously mentioned New York Times article spoke to a certain class of European that would be welcome; the report welcomed the common man, claiming that "the common people of Europe do not suffer from the ignorant prejudices that affect the aristocratic and snobocratic classes. They do not rejoice over the collapse of democracy." Furthermore the article states:

The "immigrant" coming here this year is, in general, as fine a class as ever landed upon our shores. ... Most of them are farmers, mechanics and artisans, and have come here on their way to the West. ...**They find themselves welcomed to this country**, which they know their rulers, and their Press, and their Parliamentary spouters have abused; and they find that here, even now, there is work, there is land, there is a home and plenty for all.

It was nearly universally accepted that there were more resources than people and that the West was a sufficient destination to accommodate the surplus laborers in Eastern U.S. cities as well **as the European Immigrant**. This in turn, it was believed, or at least hoped, would generate unprecedented wealth from agriculture and industry.

The result of the Homestead Act of 1862 and the effect it had on immigration is difficult to quantify in that no statistics were kept to track causation, but there is statistics that flesh out a correlation between the two. By 1870, seven years after the Homestead Act went into effect; population data highlights the immediate impact on immigration to the Great Plains.

The 1870 census reveals New York's foreign born population was 26% of the total population, the highest of any on the Atlantic Coast. However, this would have been well behind the homesteaded states of Wyoming and Montana who both had 39%, and the Dakota Territory boasted a foreign born population of 34%. Nebraska's 25% put it one percentage point behind New York. Even Kansas still had a substantial 13% of its population born in a foreign country.

The percentage of foreign born individuals in the population is further highlighted by the population increases in these states. Nebraska's population increased over 425% in the same decade from just fewer than 29,000 to seven short of 123,000. Kansas saw an increase from 107,000 to 364,000, nearly 340%, and the Dakota Territory jumped from 4,800 to 14,181, an increase in 293%. Wyoming and Montana had an official population of 0 in 1860 and by 1870 Wyoming had 9,118 and Montana leaped to 20,595.

The total population of states and territories (excluding Texas) west of the Missouri River in 1860 was 759,860, and those same states" population nearly doubled to 1,492,092 by 1870.17 The correlation does not end in the 19th century. In fact, this was evident well into the 20th century when the peak years in immigration, 1905-14, also coincides with the peak years in homestead claims.

The Homestead Act was the first of its kind to accommodate immigration and provide the necessary requirements for naturalization. The legislation went beyond simply providing an incentive to come to the United States; it integrated the components for citizenship as well. By requiring a declaration of intention to become a U.S. citizen in order to file for a homestead the first component of the naturalization process was met.

Furthermore, the Homestead Act required a 5 year residency period to ensure a potential settler would improve the land. This satisfied the second requirement in the naturalization process. No previous bill in U.S. history went so far to invite immigration and to provide a clearly defined path to citizenship.

In many respects, it protected the immigrant homesteader from potential exploitation; succeeding where other immigration law had failed. Land and immigration in the United States have been bound throughout the nation's history, so it is fitting that the first accommodating immigration law was actually a land law.

https://www.nps.gov/home/upload/Immigration-White-Paper.pdf

It can be seen that the goal of the Homestead Act was to increase the amount of European immigrants to live on American soil. Land that was illegally and erroneously taken from Aboriginal Americans (blacks, negroes, colored, African-Americans) and given to foreigners. Let's add that the people who were giving the land away had no right's to do so. This falls under the hideous Doctrine of Discovery.

It cannot be denied that the Homestead Act was to populate North America with Europeans to replace the Aboriginal American who's land it was from birth. Proof that it worked to increase immigration was that less than a month after the act was passed immigration increased.

From early on, the playing field was tipped to favor the European immigrant. While the Aboriginal American birthrights, land, and all entitlements were taken because foreigners wanted so-called religious freedom which was the first thing they denied the indigenous people. How ironic!

Due to the Doctrine of Discovery, they became second class citizens on their own land! They magically became dependent nations on the United States government. Because when the European invaders landed and didn't see any Christians, they viewed the land as unoccupied. (See The Truth of The Doctrine of Discovery by the same author) Martin Luther King in his speech on the March on Washington said, "One hundred years later, the Negro is still languishing in the corners of American society and finds himself **an exile in his own land**. So we have come here today to dramatize a shameful condition."

It wouldn't be too far of a stretch of the imagination to think that the descendants of the people who were not from North America, (European immigrants) became the primary land dwellers/owners due to their ancestors ability to claim property they didn't own or weren't entitled to initially. They were invited over by fellows of their continent initially to get first dibs on land that belonged to someone else. These are the first rumblings of what would eventually become white privilege.

How can it not be? European immigrants got an advantage. The Homestead Act was cultivated and groomed exactly for them to possess what wasn't theirs. They received a head start. This same advantage was passed down to their descendants. Who, were born on land that wasn't originally theirs, and were/have been able to receive benefits authorized for the Aboriginal American.

Identity Theft

The Dawes Act of 1887 (also known as the General Allotment Act or the Dawes Severalty Act of 1887),[1][2] authorized the

President of the United States to survey Native American tribal land and divide it into allotments for individual Native Americans. **Those who accepted allotments and lived separately from the tribe would be granted United States citizenship**. The Dawes Act was amended in 1891, in 1898 by the Curtis Act, and again in 1906 by the Burke Act.

The Act was named for its creator, Senator Henry L. Dawes of Massachusetts. The objectives of the Dawes Act were to abolish tribal and communal land ownership of the tribes into individual land ownership **rights in order to transfer lands under Native American control to white settlers and stimulate assimilation of them into mainstream American society**, and thereby lift individual Native Americans out of poverty. Individual household ownership of land and subsistence farming on the European-American model was seen as an essential step. The act provided the government would classify as "excess" those Indian reservation lands remaining after allotments, and sell those lands on the open market, allowing purchase and settlement by non-Native Americans.

During the 1850s, the United States federal government's attempt to exert control over the Native Americans expanded. **Numerous new European immigrants were settling on the eastern border of the Indian territories**, where most of the Native American tribes were situated. Conflicts between the groups increased as they competed for resources and operated according to different cultural systems. Many European Americans did not believe that members of the two racial societies could coexist within the same communities. Searching for a quick solution to their problem, William Medill the Commissioner of Indian Affairs, proposed establishing "colonies" or "reservations" that would be exclusively for the natives, similar to those which some native tribes had created for themselves in the east.

It was a form of removal, whereby the US government would uproot the natives from their current locations, to areas in the region beyond the Mississippi River. **This would enable settlement by European Americans in the Southeast in turn opening up new placement for the new white settlers** and at the same time protecting them from the corrupt "evil" ways of the subordinate natives.

The new policy intended to concentrate Native Americans in areas away from encroaching settlers, **but it caused considerable suffering and many deaths**. During the nineteenth century, Native American tribes resisted the imposition of the reservation system and engaged with the United States Army in what were called the Indian Wars in the West for decades. Finally defeated by the US military force and **continuing waves of encroaching settlers**, the tribes negotiated agreements to resettle on reservations.[6] Native Americans ended up with a total of over 155 million acres (630,000 km2) of land, ranging from arid deserts to prime agricultural land.

https://en.wikipedia.org/wiki/Dawes_Rolls

The Dawes Rolls (or Final Rolls of Citizens and Freedmen of the Five Civilized Tribes, or Dawes Commission of Final Rolls) were created by the United States Dawes Commission. The Commission was authorized by United States Congress in 1893 to execute the General Allotment Act of 1887.

Traditionally, the land in these tribal communities had been held communally. With the establishment of the Dawes Commission, the ruling was made by the colonial agents to divide up the land into parcels and institute a system of individual ownership in accordance with US laws, overriding the treaty and tribal laws of the region. In order to allot the communal lands, citizens of the Five civilized tribes (Cherokee, Choctaw, Creek, Chickasaw, and Seminole) were to be enumerated and registered by the US government. These counts also included the freedmen - formerly-enslaved African-Americans who had been emancipated after the American Civil War, and their descendants. The rolls were used to assign allotments to heads of household and to provide an equitable division of all monies obtained from sales of surplus lands. These rolls became known as the Dawes Rolls. When word got out that people could get land, **many non-Natives appeared at the offices and falsely claimed to be Native**. Most of these false claimants claimed to be Cherokee. Family myths still persist of "hiding in the hills", or of being "rejected from the rolls", or "refusing to enroll" when the reason for having not been enrolled is that the applicants were simply not Native American.

https://en.wikipedia.org/wiki/Dawes_Rolls

Dawes rolls rife with 'opportunistic white men' and early appropriation.

These so-called five-dollar Indians paid government agents under the table in order to reap the benefits that came with having Indian blood. Mainly white men with an appetite for land, five-dollar Indians paid to register on the Dawes Rolls, earning fraudulent enrollment in tribes along with benefits inherited by generations to come.

"These were opportunistic white men who wanted access to land or food rations," said Gregory Smithers, associate professor of history at Virginia Commonwealth University. "These were people who were more than happy to exploit the Dawes Commission-and government agents, for $5, were willing to turn a blind eye to the graft and corruption."

"The federal government poured a lot of effort and energy into the Dawes Commission, but at the same **time it was very hard for both Native and American governments to keep track of who was who**."

The Dawes Commission set up tents in Indian Territory, said Bill Welge, director emeritus of the Oklahoma Historical Society's Office of American Indian Culture and Preservation. There, field clerks scoured written records, took oral testimony and generated enrollment cards for individuals determined to have Indian blood.

That included **authentic Indians**, Welge said. **But it also included lots of people with questionable heritage**.

"Commissioners took advantage of their positions and **enrolled people who had very minimal or questionable connections to the tribes**," he said. "**They were not adverse to taking money under the table**."

The implications of such shady practices are enormous now, Smithers said. **Five-dollar Indians passed their unearned benefits to heirs who still lay claim to tribal citizenship and associated privileges**.

"**Now we have people who are white but who can trace their names back to the rolls used by tribal nations to ascertain who has rights as citizens**," he said. "**That means we have white people who have the ability to vote at large; it means political rights; it means the potential to influence tribal policy on a whole range of issues; it means people have access to health care, education and employment. The implications are quite profound for people who got away with fraud**.

On the flip side, while non-Natives paid to play Indian, many authentic Indians who didn't trust the government chose not to register with the Dawes Rolls at all, said Gene Norris, a genealogist at the Cherokee National Historical Society. **That means people with legitimate claims to tribal enrollment and the benefits are now excluded**.

The **Dawes Rolls-even now- are a murky and "very inaccurate" gauge of Indian citizenship**, he said. In the 2000 Census, the number of people claiming Cherokee ancestry was three times that of official tribal enrollment.

https://newsmaven.io/indiancountrytoday/archive/paying-to-play-indian-the-dawes-rolls-and-the-legacy-of-5-indians-3yha0LldYUaH7smRsrks8A/

During the late 1800's, in an effort to assimilate the Native Americans of the time into white culture the United States government passed several bills requiring the five civilized tribes (Cherokee, Choctaw, Chickasaw, Creek and Seminole) to accept specific land allotments as well as register for what was called the "Dawes Rolls".

This less than effective screening process allowed white men looking to get their hands on a piece of guaranteed land to strike a deal, paying the commissioners five dollars under the table to be placed on the Dawes Rolls. This helped coin the term "5 dollar Indian".

At the time, because of their distrust for the United States government, **a lot of full-blooded Indians didn't even bother registering on the Dawes rolls, which systematically shut them out from any future benefits**.

So, don't be surprised when you go to your favorite casino (most of which are on Indian reservations) and find one of the owners who says he is part "Cherokee." In actuality, he's nothing more than a five dollar Indian.

https://www.melanatedfathers.com/2017/10/20/the-dawes-rolls-the-making-of-a-5-dollar-indian/

Black Indians, or rather Aborigines of America, were supposed to benefit but the government gave the majority of the land, legal tenders, tax reliefs and other federal specialized benefits to white settlers; who paid-off the citizenship administrative organizations, in order to become members of what is known as the Five Civilized Tribes in Indian Territory by Congress.

White settlers sought to reap the benefits of the Aborigines. In fact, one example of that would be the complexity of how successful, but so openly fraudulent they did it.

In 1895, the white settlers were informed of what benefits the Indians were entitled to, so they traveled to the Dawes Roll Commission to inquire about having their names enlisted on the roll cards for full blooded and/or Freedman Indians of America lands.

In 1898, the Dawes Roll acted as a census responsible for documenting records of one's ethnic backgrounds, in order to determine one's association with specific American Indian tribes.

Also, it played an important role with determining which Indian tribes would get land allotments and other benefits that I detailed earlier, in return for abolishing their tribal governments and recognizing Federal laws. In order to receive the land, individual tribal members first had to apply, and then be deemed eligible by the Commission.

During the early part of the year 1902, the US Government reacted with malicious intent, in developing a separate Freedmen's list **specifically designed to rule out all 'copper colored' Indians from receiving these newly established benefits by way of the Federal Government**.

What is also important to note, the US Government listed all full blooded Indigenous Aborigines of America, mainly all of the Indians who they thought had African like features, as "Colored" as their classification of race documented inside of the 1900 Census.

Simultaneously, white U.S. citizens were allowed to become identified as Indians by paying the Dawes Commission a whopping total of just five dollars for each white adult and child to be listed on the Dawes Roll.

On April 1st, 1902, public notices were passed around, detailing that other "claimants" can legally make their cases for Freedman Enrollment.

Singlehandedly allowing all white citizens the rights to legally steal the Indian lands of America (again), reparations, and optimized benefits set fourth by Federal law. Ironically, this was officially announced on the day most people would tell their very best April Fool's jokes.

https://imjustheretomakeyouthink.com/2017/04/03/untold-history-about-the-five-dollar-indians-culture-vultures-that-inherited-billions-of-dollars-million-acres-of-indian-land/

The Red Line

Redlining--a discriminatory practice by which banks, insurance companies, etc., refuse or limit loans, mortgages, insurance, etc., within specific geographic areas, especially inner-city neighborhoods.

https://www.dictionary.com/browse/redlining

Racial discrimination in mortgage lending in the 1930s shaped the demographic and wealth patterns of American communities today, a new study shows, **with 3 out of 4 neighborhoods "redlined" on government maps 80 years ago continuing to struggle economically**.

The study by the National Community Reinvestment Coalition, released Wednesday, shows **that the vast majority of neighborhoods marked "hazardous" in red ink on maps drawn by the federal Home Owners' Loan Corp. from 1935 to 1939 are today much more likely than other areas to comprise lower-income, minority residents**.

"**It's as if some of these places have been trapped in the past, locking neighborhoods into concentrated poverty**," said Jason Richardson, director of research at the NCRC, a consumer advocacy group.

In the 1930s, government surveyors graded neighborhoods in 239 cities, color-coding them green for "best," blue for "still desirable," yellow for "definitely declining" and red for "hazardous." The "redlined" areas were the ones local lenders discounted as credit risks, in large part because of the residents' racial and ethnic demographics. They also took into account local amenities and home prices.

Neighborhoods that were predominantly made up of African Americans, as well as Catholics, Jews and immigrants from Asia and southern Europe, were deemed undesirable. “**Anyone who was not northern-European white was considered to be a detraction from the value of the area**,” said Bruce Mitchell, a senior researcher at the NCRC and one of the study’s authors.

Loans in these neighborhoods were unavailable or very expensive, **making it more difficult for low-income minorities to buy homes and setting the stage for the country’s persistent racial wealth gap**. (White families today have nearly 10 times the net worth of black families and more than eight times that of Hispanic families, according to the Federal Reserve.)

“**Homeownership is the number-one method of accumulating wealth**, but the effect of these policies that create more hurdles for the poor is a permanent underclass that’s disproportionately minority,” said John Taylor, president and chief executive of the NCRC. “I think most people believe the problem is not with the rules but with the people. Most middle-class whites in America don’t have empirical observations of what happens in underserved neighborhoods or understand the historical treatment of poor and minority communities.”

The Federal Housing Administration institutionalized the system of discriminatory lending in government-backed mortgages, reflecting local race-based criteria in their underwriting practices and reinforcing residential segregation in American cities. The discriminatory practices captured by the HOLC maps continued until 1968, when the Fair Housing Act banned racial discrimination in housing.

But 50 years after that law passed, the lingering effects of redlining are clear, with the pattern of economic and racial residential segregation still evident in many U.S. cities — from Montgomery, Ala., to Flint, Mich., to Denver.

Nationally, **nearly two-thirds of neighborhoods deemed "hazardous" are inhabited by mostly minority residents, typically black and Latino**, researchers found. Cities with more such neighborhoods have significantly greater economic inequality. On the flip side, 91 percent of areas classified as "best" in the 1930s remain middle-to-upper-income today, and 85 percent of them are still predominantly white.

https://www.washingtonpost.com/news/wonk/wp/2018/03/28/redlining-was-banned-50-years-ago-its-still-hurting-minorities-today/?utm_term=.2a1bb82ffd50

But instead of using these maps only for HOLC refinances, which would have been racist in and of itself, banks began using these maps for all home purchases and refinances. Again, with Jim Crow segregation in place, blacks couldn't simply move to the non-redlined, white neighborhoods. **So, because of this, as generations of Americans lifted themselves out of poverty, black people could not take part in the primary driver of wealth, homeownership**.

Redlining was outlawed in 1968 by the Fair Housing Act, but it still affects almost every economic aspect of black communities to this day.

The University of Richmond has compiled high-resolution images of the original redlining maps, and it is startling to see how much they reflect the racial, economic and wealth disparities in cities across America.

Residents who live in redlined areas pay higher interest rates and are denied mortgages more often than whites with the same credit and income, according to reporting for the Center for Investigative Journalism. **People in redlined areas pay higher auto insurance rates**, ProPublica reports. Homes in black neighborhoods are valued, on average, $48,000 less than homes in white neighborhoods with similar crime rates and amenities.

According to the Lincoln Institute of Land Policy, about 36 percent of education funding comes from local property taxes. **These lower home values, which are the direct result of redlining, means that schools in black neighborhoods receive less funding**. This is why, according to a 2019 study by Edbuild, schools serving nonwhite students receive $23 billion less in funding than majority-white schools despite serving the same number of students. It's why the average nonwhite school district receives $2,226 less per student than a white school district.

Because poverty, education, or lack thereof, and crime rates are interrelated, it makes sense that black children, who are more likely to live in undervalued homes inside underfunded school districts, are also more vulnerable to the criminal justice system. This is the real school-to-prison pipeline.

Even though blacks and whites use drugs at about the same rate, blacks are three times more likely to be arrested for possession of an illegal substance. This is partly because **police patrol formerly redlined areas and make more drug arrests**. In Baltimore, maps of poverty, drug arrests and police shootings are nearly identical and are almost totally contained within the boundaries of formerly redlined areas. A study by the state of Maryland Public Defenders Office also found that 13 of the 15 zip codes where suspects routinely receive higher bail amounts were in redlined areas.

Aside from crime, education and economics, redlining still affects black people in numerous ways. **People in redlined neighborhoods wait longer to vote, are disproportionately disenfranchised, wait longer for emergency services, receive more parking violations, and have less access to fresh food**.

These things are not a coincidence. They all stem from the fact that black people have been denied access to intergenerational wealth building by a government policy that is interwoven into the fabric of American society. This nation became an international economic superpower because it was built on the foundation of slavery.

https://www.theroot.com/redlining-the-origin-story-of-institutional-racism-1834308539

The government's efforts were "primarily designed to provide housing to white, middle-class, lower-middle-class families," he says. **African-Americans and other people of color were left out of the new suburban communities — and pushed instead into urban housing projects**.

Rothstein's new book, The Color of Law, examines the local, state and federal housing policies that mandated segregation. He notes that the Federal Housing Administration, which was established in 1934, **furthered the segregation efforts by refusing to insure mortgages in and near African-American neighborhoods** — a policy known as "redlining." **At the same time, the FHA was subsidizing builders who were mass-producing entire subdivisions for whites — with the requirement that none of the homes be sold to African-Americans**.

Rothstein says these decades-old housing policies have had a lasting effect on American society. "The segregation of our metropolitan areas today leads ... **to stagnant inequality, because families are much less able to be upwardly mobile when they're living in segregated neighborhoods where opportunity is absent**," he says. "If we want greater equality in this society, if we want a lowering of the hostility between police and young African-American men, we need to take steps to desegregate."

The Federal Housing Administration's justification was that if African-Americans bought homes in these suburbs, or even if they bought homes near these suburbs, the property values of the homes they were insuring, the white homes they were insuring, would decline. And therefore their loans would be at risk.

There was no basis for this claim on the part of the Federal Housing Administration. In fact, when African-Americans tried to buy homes in all-white neighborhoods or in mostly white neighborhoods, property values rose because African-Americans were more willing to pay more for properties than whites were, simply because their housing supply was so restricted and they had so many fewer choices. So the rationale that the Federal Housing Administration used was never based on any kind of study. It was never based on any reality.

It was in something called the Underwriting Manual of the Federal Housing Administration, which said that "**incompatible racial groups should not be permitted to live in the same communities." Meaning that loans to African-Americans could not be insured**.

In one development ... in Detroit ... the FHA would not go ahead, during World War II, with this development unless the developer built a 6-foot-high wall, cement wall, separating his development from a nearby African-American neighborhood to make sure that no African-Americans could even walk into that neighborhood.

The Underwriting Manual of the Federal Housing Administration recommended that highways be a good way to separate African-American from white neighborhoods. So this was not a matter of law, it was a matter of government regulation, but it also wasn't hidden, so it can't be claimed that this was some kind of "de facto" situation. Regulations that are written in law and published ... in the Underwriting Manual are as much a de jure unconstitutional expression of government policy as something written in law.

So in 1968 we passed the Fair Housing Act that said, in effect, "OK, African-Americans, you're now free to buy homes in Daly City or Levittown" ... but it's an empty promise because those homes are no longer affordable to the families that could've afforded them when whites were buying into those suburbs and gaining the equity and the wealth that followed from that.

The white families sent their children to college with their home equities; they were able to take care of their parents in old age and not depend on their children. They're able to bequeath wealth to their children. None of those advantages accrued to African-Americans, who for the most part were prohibited from buying homes in those suburbs.

Public housing began in this country for civilians during the New Deal and it was an attempt to address a housing shortage; it wasn't a welfare program for poor people. During the Depression, no housing construction was going on. Middle-class families, working-class families were losing their homes during the Depression when they became unemployed and so there were many unemployed middle-class, working-class white families and this was the constituency that the federal government was most interested in. And so the federal government began a program of building public housing for whites only in cities across the country. The liberal instinct of some Roosevelt administration officials led them to build some projects for African-Americans as well, but they were always separate projects; they were not integrated. ...

The white projects had large numbers of vacancies; black projects had long waiting lists. Eventually it became so conspicuous that the public housing authorities in the federal government opened up the white-designated projects to African-Americans, and they filled with African-Americans. At the same time, industry was leaving the cities, African-Americans were becoming poorer in those areas, the projects became projects for poor people, not for working-class people. They became subsidized, they hadn't been subsidized before. ... And so they became vertical slums that we came to associate with public housing. ...

The vacancies in the white projects were created primarily by the Federal Housing Administration program to suburbanize America, and the Federal Housing Administration subsidized mass production builders to create subdivisions that were "white-only" and they subsidized the families who were living in the white housing projects as well as whites who were living elsewhere in the central city to move out of the central cities and into these white-only suburbs. So it was the Federal Housing Administration that depopulated public housing of white families, while the public housing authorities were charged with the responsibility of housing African-Americans who were increasingly too poor to pay the full cost of their rent.

https://www.npr.org/2017/05/03/526655831/a-forgotten-history-of-how-the-u-s-government-segregated-america

What do you think? Do white people have privilege?

All emphasis is mine.

www.ingramcontent.com/pod-product-compliance
Ingram Content Group UK Ltd.
Pitfield, Milton Keynes, MK11 3LW, UK
UKHW051135260726
13967UKWH00010B/3070

9 780359 712519